hjbnf
616.2414 WILL

W9-BWN-030

DISCARD

Williams, Heather DiLorenzo, autho
A lasting impact
33410016849178   12-09-2020

Hebron Public Library
201 W. Sigler Street
Hebron, IN 46341

COVID-19

A Lasting Impact

by Heather DiLorenzo Williams

LERNER PUBLICATIONS ◆ MINNEAPOLIS

Copyright © 2021 by Lerner Publishing Group, Inc.

All rights reserved. International copyright secured. No part of this book may be reproduced, stored in a retrieval system, or transmitted in any form or by any means—electronic, mechanical, photocopying, recording, or otherwise—without the prior written permission of Lerner Publishing Group, Inc., except for the inclusion of brief quotations in an acknowledged review.

Lerner Publications Company
An imprint of Lerner Publishing Group, Inc.
241 First Avenue North
Minneapolis, MN 55401 USA

For reading levels and more information, look up this title at www.lernerbooks.com.

All facts and data represented in this book were accurate according to sources available as of May 2020.

Image credits: Zimniy/Shutterstock, p. 1; kenny hung photography/Getty Images, p. 3 (bottom left); Paulus Rusyanto/ EyeEm/Getty Images, p. 3 (bottom right); Shaw Photography Co./Getty Images, p. 3 (top); Pordee_Aomboon/ Shutterstock, p. 3 (middle); Stringer/Getty Images, p. 5; Marco Di Lauro/Getty Images, p. 6; Scott Eisen/Getty Images, p. 7 (top); anucha sirivisansuwan/Shutterstock, p. 7 (bottom); Joe Raedle/Getty Images, p. 8; Alex Wong/Getty Images, p. 9 (right); Suttipong Sutiratanachai/Getty Images, p. 9 (left); David Dee Delgado/Getty Images, p. 11; Ariel Skelley/Getty Images, p. 12; Al Drago/Bloomberg/Getty Images, p. 13; Alex Wong/Getty Images, p. 14; Abscent/ Shutterstock, p. 15; Kevin Frayer/Getty Images, p. 17; kenny hung photography/Getty Images, p. 18 (left); Jose Gil/ Shutterstock, p. 18 (right); Marco Di Lauro/Getty Images, p. 19 (top); valentinrussanov/Getty Images, p. 19 (bottom); Shaw Photography Co./Getty Images, p. 20; Aleks47/Shutterstock, p. 21 (electricity); grmarc/Shutterstock, p. 21 (recycle symbol); Irina Strelnikova/Shutterstock, p. 21 (volunteers); Marnikus/Shutterstock, p. 21 (water); Neonic Flower/ Shutterstock, p. 21 (bee); WilleeCole Photography/Shutterstock, p. 21 (reusable bag); Pordee_Aomboon/Shutterstock, p. 23; Ariel Skelley/Getty Images, p. 24; Leremy/Shutterstock, p. 25 (hugging); naum/Shutterstock, p. 25; popicon/ Shutterstock, p. 25 (tissue); Al Bello/Getty Images, p. 26; Joe Raedle/Getty Images, p. 27; Ariel Skelley/Getty Images, p. 28 (middle); Stringer/Getty Images, p. 28 (top); valentinrussanov/Getty Images, p. 28 (bottom); Background: gaisonok/ Getty Images; Cover: Zimniy/Shutterstock (top); SvetaZi/Getty Images (bottom); Fact icon: sinisamaric1/Pixabay

Main body text set in Minion Pro.
Typeface provided by Adobe Originals.

Editor: Lauren Dupuis-Perez **Designer**: Deron Payne

Library of Congress Cataloging-in-Publication Data
The Cataloging-in-Publication Data for *COVID-19: A Lasting Impact* is on file at the Library of Congress.
ISBN 978-1-72842-799-7 (lib. bdg.)

Manufactured in the United States of America
Corporate Graphics, North Mankato, MN

CONTENTS

Shutting Down the World

The first case of COVID-19 was in China. It happened in late 2019. The illness spread through the country quickly. Some **provinces** in China were placed under **quarantine**. Markets and restaurants closed. People were not allowed to leave their homes.

By February 2020, it was clear that the virus had spread to other countries. Italy was one. Everyone in Italy was on lockdown by the middle of March. This meant they could only leave their homes for food and medicine. People in some places could not even go outside.

The illness became a global pandemic. This means it is an illness affecting the whole world. Most countries were given stay-at-home orders. This would help slow the spread of COVID-19. By the end of March, more than one-third of the world's population was required to stay home.

DID YOU KNOW?
A Chinese doctor named Li Wenliang was the first person to warn the medical community about COVID-19. He died from the virus on February 7, 2020.

province: an area or region of a country

quarantine: keeping a person away from others to stop the spread of disease

China was the first country to shut down because of COVID-19.

World Shutdowns

COVID-19 led to stay-at-home orders. These were a little different for each country. Some countries only allowed people to leave home at set times each day. In other places, people could only go out on certain days of the week.

Many cities around the world closed **nonessential** businesses. Hospitals and pharmacies stayed open. Grocery stores also stayed open. But in many places, factories stopped running. They stopped making and selling products. **Recreational** events were closed or canceled. This included live music, plays, movies, and sports. The 2020 Summer Olympics were moved to 2021. It was the first time in history that the Olympics were **postponed**.

On March 9, Italy began a nationwide quarantine. Normally busy streets were empty as people stayed in their homes.

nonessential: not required

recreational: related to activities done for fun, such as sports or hobbies

postpone: to change to a time later than originally scheduled

Many countries had travel bans. They closed their borders and did not allow people in or out. Flights from other countries were canceled. People all over the world postponed vacations. Many people stopped driving to work. Since there was less travel, people were not using as much gasoline. Companies that made gas had too much. Gas prices dropped very low.

During the shutdown, airlines around the United States reported a 96 percent decrease in travelers.

ALL FILLED UP AND NO PLACE TO GO

Gas is made from oil. In April of 2020, 27 full oil tankers docked off the coast of California. They held about 20 percent of the normal amount of oil used worldwide each day. At that time, oil storage units around the world were full. Those tankers became floating storage units. They docked until they had a place to empty their oil.

As the COVID-19 crisis continued, toilet paper became one of the hardest-to-find items.

US Shutdown

In March 2020, the Centers for Disease Control and Prevention (CDC) told people to stay home. Many schools across the country closed. By early April, most states had official stay-at-home orders. Many people started working from home. Others lost their jobs.

Parks and beaches closed during the shutdown. Kids were not allowed to play on playgrounds. Youth sports teams stopped practicing. The National Basketball Association season paused. Major League Baseball was postponed.

Some people panicked. They started to **stockpile** medicine, cleaning products, and some paper products. Stores ran out of many items. Other people disagreed with the stay-at-home orders. They gathered in large groups. They wanted to go back to work. Even though the illness continued to spread, people still disagreed about what was best.

stockpile: to store items, such as food, to be saved for future use

Key Shutdown Dates Worldwide

LATE 2019
China reports a number of mysterious pneumonia cases. They were all connected to the same seafood market in the city of Wuhan.

JANUARY 23, 2020
The Chinese province of Hubei, which includes Wuhan, is placed under quarantine.

MARCH 9, 2020
Italy's leaders announce that all 60 million residents of Italy are under lockdown.

MARCH 11, 2020
US President Donald Trump bans travel into the US from all 26 European countries.

MARCH 19, 2020
California becomes the first US state to issue a stay-at-home order to its residents.

MARCH 31, 2020
More than one-third of the world is under some form of lockdown.

APRIL 7, 2020
Around 95 percent of Americans in 42 US states are under some form of stay-at-home order.

APRIL 30, 2020
Georgia becomes the first US state to lift its stay-at-home orders, against CDC recommendations.

APRIL 8, 2020
China lifts the lockdown in the area where the first case of COVID-19 was detected.

A Shut-Down Economy

The economy is the way people make and spend money. It is made of buyers and sellers. Most people are both. People spend money to buy items such as food, clothing, and cars. They also buy services. Yard work and fixing cars are examples of services. People who do this kind of work are selling a service. People also sell houses, cars, and things they make.

There are local economies and state economies. Each country has a national economy. People and businesses all over the globe make up the world economy.

Buying and selling keeps money moving. This creates a good economy. The COVID-19 shutdown led to a bad economy. People did not spend as much. They were not going to the movies because theaters were closed. They were not eating in restaurants. Most stores were closed, so people could not go shopping for clothes or shoes. This meant less money was being spent.

DID YOU KNOW?

Coins were first used to purchase items in what is now Turkey. This was around the 5th or 6th century BCE. The first country to use paper money was China.

Many stores boarded up windows during the shutdown to prevent theft.

In some neighborhoods, robots deliver groceries to homes.

COVID-19 and Businesses

Online companies like Amazon and Netflix kept making money during the shutdown. People were still buying things online. They kept watching movies. But many small and local businesses struggled. The CARES Act helped some of them. Others had to be creative. They had to find ways to keep making money.

Many people were nervous about going to stores. Grocery stores and pharmacies started delivering to people's homes. Restaurants had to close their dining areas. They sold food as takeout or delivery instead. Waiters and waitresses became delivery drivers. Gyms and exercise studios started offering online classes. Many shops started selling items online.

These methods worked to keep some businesses running. Unfortunately, millions of businesses may not be able to reopen when the COVID-19 shutdown is over.

CARES Act Funding: Where Did It Go?

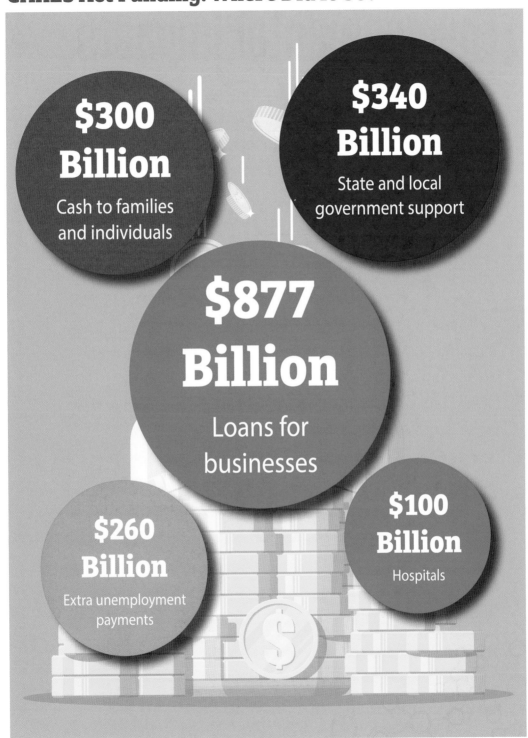

$300 Billion
Cash to families and individuals

$340 Billion
State and local government support

$877 Billion
Loans for businesses

$260 Billion
Extra unemployment payments

$100 Billion
Hospitals

Environmental Impacts

Air pollution has been a big problem in the world for many years. Human activities cause air pollution. Cars and planes release smoke and fumes. Factories also create air pollution. This is called smog. The air quality in many large cities is bad.

Scientists learned that bad air quality made COVID-19 worse. People who lived in places with bad air quality had a hard time getting well. Their lungs were already working hard to breathe. COVID-19 made breathing harder.

Then countries began to shut down. People stayed home. Cars and planes were not using gas. The air started to get clearer and cleaner. Scientists have discovered that the COVID-19 shutdown did more than stop the spread of the virus. It also helped the environment.

DID YOU KNOW?

Air inside homes is two to five times more polluted than outside air. A few causes of indoor air pollution are smoking, some appliances, and mold. Opening a window can clear the air of these **toxins**.

toxin: a poisonous substance

Air pollution can increase the risk of heart disease, stroke, and lung diseases. Children and older people are impacted the most.

Air Quality

The air quality in Los Angeles, California, is usually very bad. It is one of the most polluted cities in the US. Most of LA's smog is caused by cars. Some is caused by **freight** ships in nearby ports. Some is also caused by factories.

The COVID-19 shutdown forced people in LA to stay home. There was less traffic. Fewer planes were flying. People started walking or biking to the store. The skies over LA started to clear. During March of 2020, LA had 21 days of good air quality. The city's air quality had not been that good in more than forty years.

---

freight: goods shipped from one place to another

In 2019, Los Angeles was named the smoggiest city in the United States.

In March 2020, residents of Venice, Italy, shared photos of empty canals where the water was clear and fish could be seen swimming around.

Other places around the world also had better air quality during the shutdown. Cities in China, India, and Italy had less smog. But factories won't be closed forever. People will start driving and traveling again. Humans will have to make big changes if they want the air to stay clean.

KEEPING THE AIR CLEAN

Trees and plants help keep the air outside clean. This is one way people can help keep the air clean once the COVID-19 shutdown ends. One tree can remove between 10 and 50 pounds of pollution from the air. If every family in the US planted a new tree, air pollution on Earth could go down by about 5 percent.

Wildlife

The COVID-19 shutdown has also been good for wildlife. People are driving less. This means fewer animals are being hit by cars. Some cities are not cutting the grass along roads. This has allowed more wildflowers to grow. More flowers attract honeybees, which help **pollinate** fruits and vegetables.

Many beaches closed because of COVID-19. Leatherback sea turtles have been better able to lay their eggs. There are no people to disturb them. Scientists think more eggs could hatch if there is less activity on the beach.

The shutdown has even been good for homeless pets. In some areas, the number of pet adoptions rose. Shelters in California and Illinois posted photos of empty cages on their social media accounts. All of their animals had been adopted or **fostered**.

The American Society for the Prevention of Cruelty to Animals has reported a 70 percent increase in families offering to foster animals in New York and Los Angeles.

pollinate: to move pollen from flower to flower to help plants make seeds

foster: when a pet is cared for by someone who is not the owner

Protecting Our Planet Starts with You

Use less electricity.
Turn off the lights and other electronics when you aren't using them.

Waste less.
Reduce trash and recycle glass, paper, and plastic.

Save water.
Don't let the water run when you're brushing your teeth, and check your house for leaks.

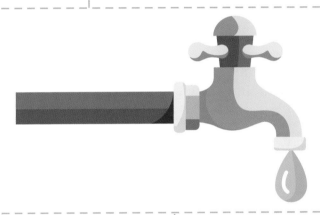

Volunteer.
Pick up trash around your neighborhood or clean up a local stream or river.

Feed the birds and the bees!
Buy or make bird feeders and plant bee-friendly flowers.

Use fewer single-use items.
Buy reusable shopping bags, lunch bags, straws, and water bottles.

Looking Toward the Future

The COVID-19 pandemic has been a scary time for the whole world. It has changed the way we do many things. But many believe it could help people create a better future.

Some countries were not ready for a global pandemic. COVID-19 could help world leaders be more prepared in the future. Having a plan in place is important. People handle a crisis better when their leaders have a good plan. Having enough medical supplies is also important. COVID-19 has shown that it is important to have the space, equipment, and workers to treat sick patients.

Leaders can also take steps to contain future pandemics. This means stopping viruses from spreading to so many people. Scientists are learning more about how to stop the spread of COVID-19 every day.

MAKING A VACCINE

A vaccine is a kind of medicine. Vaccines stop viruses or bacteria from **replicating**. Vaccines contain a tiny bit of a germ. When the germ enters the body, the body makes **antibodies**. These stay in the body. When the real germ enters the body, the antibodies are ready to fight it. Scientists started working on a COVID-19 vaccine as soon as they discovered the virus.

replicate: to make an exact copy of something, such as a cell inside the body

antibody: a substance in the body that fights against infection and disease

The more protection medical staff have, the more people will be available to help sick patients.

Better Health

COVID-19 could help people be more prepared for sickness. Better **hygiene** habits stop the spread of germs. Practicing now could help people stay well during future cold and flu seasons.

Scientists all over the world have been studying people's **immune systems**. They have been trying to understand how the body reacts to COVID-19. This helps them make tests to see how the body fights the virus. It may also help them make treatments for people who get sick with other viruses.

Many people hope the pandemic will lead to better working conditions. More employers could let people work from home. More meetings could take place online. These changes would also be good for the environment. If fewer people are driving to work, there would be less air pollution. This would help both humans and the environment.

Working from home helps create more flexible workdays and makes for a better work-life balance.

hygiene: the practice of keeping yourself and your surroundings clean

immune system: the parts of the human body that protect against germs and diseases

SLOW THE SPREAD OF COVID-19

 When coughing or sneezing, cover your nose and mouth with a tissue or your elbow.

 Dispose of used tissues properly after use.

 Regularly wash your hands with soap and warm water.

 If you have flu-like symptoms, seek medical attention immediately.

 If you have flu-like symptoms, stay at least 6 feet (1.8 meters) away from other people.

 If you have flu-like symptoms, stay home from work, school, or crowded places.

 Avoid hugging, kissing, or shaking hands when greeting.

 Avoid touching your eyes, nose, or mouth with unwashed hands.

Working Together

One positive result of the COVID-19 pandemic has been kindness. A crisis can bring people together. Helping others boosts people's mental health. This has been true during the COVID-19 shutdown. Families have made masks for neighbors and medical workers. People have taken food to older people in their neighborhoods. Whole cities have stopped everything to clap for doctors and nurses once a day. People have looked for new ways to connect with friends and family.

People in many major cities often cheer for nurses at shift change. This happens around 7:00 pm or 8:00 pm every day.

DID YOU KNOW?

Restaurants across the US are giving away free and discounted food for essential workers, including nurses, doctors, and first responders. Starbucks gave essential workers a free drink every day between March 25 and May 3, 2020.

Volunteers in Florida have prepared food boxes for those who don't have enough to eat.

Many people believe this pattern of kindness will continue. Communities will better appreciate essential workers. People will place more value on time with friends and family. In many ways, COVID-19 showed people everywhere what they needed to do better. As the virus made its way across the world, people started to make changes. From healthy habits to scientific studies to better attitudes, people's response to COVID-19 could change the world for the better.

QUIZ

1. When did President Trump ban travel from Europe to the US?

2. What two activities make up the economy?

3. What country was the first to use paper money?

4. What is the full name of the CARES Act?

5. What is smog?

6. Why did air quality around the world improve during the COVID-19 shutdown?

7. What do vaccines do to help the body fight off viruses and bacteria?

8. How much money did the US government spend on the CARES Act?

8. $2 trillion
7. They help make antibodies
6. Fewer people were traveling, fewer factories were running
5. Smoke and fumes from cars and factories
4. Coronavirus Aid, Relief, and Economic Security Act
3. China
2. Buying and selling
1. March 11, 2020

CREATE A FAMILY GRATITUDE BOARD

The COVID-19 shutdown forced many families to stop doing things they enjoyed, such as going to movies, playing team sports, and visiting with friends. Many made lists of what they were thankful for to help them keep a positive attitude during the shutdown. Help your family create a gratitude board to remind you of the things that helped you survive the shutdown, and the things you looked forward to doing when it was over.

MATERIALS

- Poster board, a large canvas, or a corkboard
- Index cards or paper cut into small squares
- Markers
- Photos of family and friends
- Pictures cut from magazines
- Glue, pushpins, or tape

STEPS

1. Call a family meeting. Make one family member the secretary. This person will take notes.
2. Talk with family members about what everyone is grateful for. Have the secretary make a list.
3. Have family members gather items that show what they are thankful for. These could be photos, drawings, or notes.
4. Attach your items to the board and talk about why you are including each one.
5. Place the board in a part of your house that everyone can see. Add new items as you think of them. Let the board remind you to appreciate the things, activities, and people you love most!

INDEX